Morning Motivation

Morning Motivation

Brandon Michael LoMeo

Printed in the United State of America
First printing October 2018

INTRODUCTION

Lacking motivation? Life throwing too many curve balls at you? I know how you feel, I've been there! When I graduated Monmouth University 9 years ago I thought the rest of my life was going to look something like this: Get a job using my degree, make money, move out of my parents house, get married by 25 and live happily ever after. Not even close, I was way off!

Life threw a lot of curve balls at me, but I knocked every single one of them out of the park and kept moving forward. I learned that motivation is the driving force behind success. It's a merciless world out there and staying motivated can be difficult with all the obstacles life throws at you. Every morning on social media I share words and wisdom to help people stay motivated. It's amazing how a few words can connect with someone and give them the motivation they need to keep moving forward.

"Morning Motivation" is a collection of thoughts, words, ideas and insight from people who have been there before and came out on top. Pick up this book whenever you need extra motivation to start your mornings!

Explore. Dream. Discover.

- Mark Twain

Victory is in having done your best. If you've done your best, you've won.

- Bill Bowerman

Too often in life, something happens, and we blame other people for us not being happy or satisfied or fulfilled. So, the point is, we all have choices, and we make the choice to accept people or situations or to not accept situations.

- Tom Brady

If the people around you make you unhappy, it's not their fault. It's your fault. They're in your professional or personal life because you drew them to you and you let them remain.

- Steve Jobs

We get one opportunity in life, one chance at life to do whatever you're going to do and lay your foundation and make whatever mark you're going to make. Whatever legacy you're going to leave; leave your legacy!

- Ray Lewis

Today I will do what others won't, so tomorrow I can accomplish what others can't.

- Jerry Rice

Believe in yourself and you will be unstoppable.

- Emily Guay

When you're different, sometimes you don't see the millions of people who accept you for what you are. All you notice is the person who doesn't.

- Jodi Picoult

As soon as you trust yourself, you will know how to live.

- Johann Wolfgang von Goethe

Don't waste your energy trying to change opinions ... Do your thing, and don't care if they like it.

- Tina Fey

Whenever you see a successful person, you only see the public glories, never the private sacrifices to reach them.

- Vaibhay Shah

If it wasn't hard, everyone would do it. It's the hard that makes it great.

- Tom Hanks

Don't wait until everything is just right. It will never be perfect. There will always be challenges, obstacles, and less than perfect conditions. So, what? Get started now. With each step you take, you will grow stronger and stronger, more and more skilled, more and more self-confident, and more and more successful.

- Mark Victor Hansen

When I started counting my blessings, my whole life turned around.

- Willie Nelson

Sweat equity is the most valuable equity there is. Know your business and industry better than anyone else in the world. Love what you do or don't do it.

- Mark Cuban

If you are insecure, guess what? The rest of the world is too. Do not overestimate the competition and underestimate yourself. You are better than you think.

- T. Harveker

Don't fake it 'til you make it. It's a lie to yourself and everyone around you. If you feel like you need to fake it, then you should check yourself.

- Travis Kalanick

Change is the law of life. And those who look only to the past or the present are certain to miss the future.

- John F Kennedy

Skills are cheap. Passion is priceless.

- Gary Vaynerchuck

Dream audaciously. Have the courage to fail forward. Act with urgency.

- Phil Knight

If you don't like something, change it. If you can't change it, change your attitude.

- Maya Angelou

For me, winning isn't something that happens suddenly on the field when the whistle blows and the crowds roar. Winning is something that builds physically and mentally every day that you train and every night that you dream.

- Emmitt Smith

Life is like riding a bicycle. To keep your balance, you must keep moving.

- Albert Einstein

The less you respond to negative people, the more peaceful your life will become.

- Buddha

The secret of getting ahead is getting started. The secret of getting started is breaking your complex overwhelming tasks into small manageable tasks and starting on the first one.

- Mark Twain

Always be yourself, because not much left in this world is unique, but you are.

- Shannon Harris

Determination silences doubters.

- Kobe Bryant

One day, you might look up and see me playing the game at 50. Don't laugh. Never say Never, because limits, like fears, are often just an illusion.

- Michael Jordan

Winning isn't getting ahead of others. It's getting ahead of yourself.

- Roger Staubach

For me, winning isn't something that happens suddenly on the field when the whistle blows and the crowds roar. Winning is something that builds physically and mentally every day that you train and every night that you dream.

- Brett Favre

We all have ability. The difference is how we use it.

- Stevie Wonder

You were not born
a winner, and you
were not born a
loser. You are
what you make
yourself to be.

- Lou Holtz

Procrastination is one of the most common and deadliest of diseases and its toll on success and happiness is heavy.

- Wayne Gretzky

There are three ways
to ultimate success:
The first way is
to be kind.
The second way is
to be kind.
The third way is
to be kind.

- Frank Rogers

The person who sends out positive thoughts activates the world around him positively and draws back to himself positive results.

- Peale

You can make something of your life. It just depends on your drive.

- Eminem

Hard work beats talent when talent doesn't work hard.

- Tim Notke

What is the point of being on this Earth if you are going to be like everyone else?

- Arnold Schwarzenegger

The quality of a person's life is in direct proportion to their commitment to excellence, regardless of their chosen field of endeavor.

- Vince Lombardi

Focus on effort, not winning. Winning is a byproduct of effort.

- John Wooden

When at a young age you learn to face your fears, that makes the difference between people being champions and people not being champions.

- Evander Holyfield

In the end, the most important thing is to be true to yourself and those you love and work hard.

- Michael Jackson

Success isn't always about 'Greatness', it's about consistency. Consistent, hard work gains success. Greatness will come.

- Dwayne Johnson

The most rewarding things you do in life are often the ones that look like they cannot be done.

- Arnold Palmer

Find something you're passionate about and keep tremendously interested in it.

- Julia Child

If you don't practice you don't deserve to win.

- Andre Agassi

I am not going
to be a star.
I am going to
be a legend.

- Freddie Mercury

You have to do something in your life that is honorable and not cowardly if you are to live in peace with yourself.

- Larry Brown

There may be people that have more talent than you, but there's no excuse for anyone to work harder than you do.

- Derek Jeter

When you've got something to prove, there's nothing greater than a challenge.

- Terry Bradshaw

During my 18 years I came to bat almost 10,000 times. I struck out about 1,700 times and walked maybe 1,800 times. You figure a ballplayer will average about 500 at bats a season. That means I played seven years without ever hitting the ball.

- Mickey Mantle

I hated every minute of training, but I said, 'Don't quit. Suffer now and live the rest of your life as a champion.'

- Muhammad Ali

There are only two options regarding commitment. You're either in or you're out. There is no such thing as life in-between.

- Pat Riley

We all have dreams. But in order to make dreams come into reality, it takes an awful lot of determination, dedication, self-discipline, and effort.

- Jesse Owens

Excellence is never an accident. It is always the result of high intention, sincere effort, and intelligent execution; it represents the wise choice of many alternatives - choice, not chance, determines your destiny.

- Aristotle

Simplify your life. Don't waste the years struggling for things that are unimportant. Don't burden yourself with possessions. Keep your needs and wants simple and enjoy what you have. Don't destroy your peace of mind by looking back, worrying about the past. Live in the present. Simplify!

- Henry David Thoreau

It takes 20 years to build a reputation and five minutes to ruin it. If you think about that, you'll do things differently.

- Warren Buffet

Discipline is the bridge between goals and accomplishment.

- Jim Rohn

Tomorrow is
my exam, but I don't
care because a single
sheet of paper can't
decide my future.

- Thomas A. Edison

A great man is hard on himself; a small man is hard on others.

- Confucius

Don't let negative and toxic people rent space in your head. Raise the rent and kick them out.

- Zig Ziglar

You were born to be real, not to be perfect. You are here to be you, not to live someone else's life.

- Ralph Marston

I can't change the fact that my paintings don't sell. But the time will come when people will recognize that they are worth more than the value of the paints used in the picture.

- Vincent Van Gogh

Intelligence without ambition is a bird without wings.

- Salvador Dali

Watch your thoughts,
they become words.
Watch your words,
they become actions.
Watch your actions,
they become habit.

- Laozi

If you don't go after what you want, you'll never have it. If you don't ask, the answer is always no. If you don't step forward, you're always in the same place.

- Nora Roberts

A lifetime of training for just ten seconds.

- Jesse Owens

The best investment you can make, is an investment in yourself...The more you learn, the more you'll earn.

- Warren Buffett

If you always put limits on everything you do, physical or anything else, it will spread into your work and into your life. There are no limits. There are only plateaus, and you must not stay there, you must go beyond them.

- Bruce Lee

It was my father who told me that there is no rapper who is singing and rapping. He told me that in order to be successful you're going to have to do something different than what everyone else is doing.

- Drake

I've done a lot of work to get where I'm at, but I have to keep working.

- Wiz Khalifa

To give anything less than your best, is to sacrifice the gift.

- Steve Prefontaine

All the adversity I've had in my life, all my troubles and obstacles, have strengthened me.... You may not realize it when it happens, but a kick in the teeth may be the best thing in the world for you.

- Walt Disney

Strive for excellence, exceed yourself, love your friend, speak the truth, practice fidelity and honor your father and mother. These principles will help you to master yourself, make you strong, give you hope and put you on the path to greatness.

- Joe Weider

Luck has nothing to do with it, because I have spent many, many hours, countless hours, on the court working for my one moment in time, not knowing when it would come.

- Serena Williams

You have to be able to accept failure to get better.

- Lebron James

Be the best version of yourself in anything you do. You don't have to live anybody else's story.

- Stephen Curry

Success represents the 1% of your work which results from the 99% that is called failure. Instead of being afraid of the challenge and failure, be afraid of avoiding the challenge and doing nothing.

- Soichiro Honda

Effort is one of those things that gives meaning to life. Effort means you care about something, that something is important to you and you are willing to work for it.

- Carol Dweck

You've got to get up every morning with determination if you're going to go to bed with satisfaction.

- George Horace Lorimer

There are always going to be obstacles that come in your way, stay positive.

- Michael Phelps

The danger is not to set your goal too high and fail to reach it. It's to set your goal too low and reach it.

- Georges St-Pierre

You can waste your
life drawing lines.
Or you can live your
life crossing them.

-Shonda Rhimes

Be patient with yourself. Self-growth is tender; it's holy ground. There's no greater investment.

-Stephen Covey

I'd rather regret the things I've done than regret the things I haven't done.

-Lucille Ball

Move out of your comfort zone. You can only grow if you are willing to feel awkward and uncomfortable when you try something new.

-Brian Tracy

The life you live is more important than the words you speak.

- Mac Miller

Don't let winning make you soft. Don't let losing make you quit. Don't let your teammates down in any situation.

-Larry Bird

A trophy carries dust. Memories last forever.

- Mary Lou Retton

My motto was always to keep swinging. Whether I was in a slump or feeling badly or having trouble off the field, the only thing to do was keep swinging.

- Hank Aaron

As strong as my legs are, it is my mind that has made me a champion.

-Michael Johnson

Life is a journey that can lead you to anywhere you want to go as long as you believe in yourself. It may be difficult, but we are our most powerful resource. The heart and the mind can and will get you through anything in life.

- Bruce Buffer

I think that
the good and
the great are only
separated by the
willingness to
sacrifice.

- Kareem Abdul-Jabbar

If you are worried about what someone is saying about you-those words will take away from you what you are setting forth to accomplish in preparing for and trying to make the team or trying to make a certain spot. My advice is to have confidence and believe in yourself!

- Julian Edelman

Winners, I am convinced, imagine their dreams first. They want it with all their heart and expect it to come true. There is, I believe, no other way to live.

- Joe Montana

Courage doesn't mean you don't get afraid. Courage means you don't let fear stop you.

- Bethany Hamilton

Stay focused. Your start does not determine how you're going to finish.

- Herm Edwards

At the end of the day, you are in control of your own happiness. Life is going to happen whether you overthink it, overstress it or not. Just experience life and be happy along the way. You can't control everything in your life, but you can control your happiness.

- Holly Holm

If you can't fly, then run.
If you can't run, then
walk. If you can't walk,
then crawl, but
whatever you do, you
have to keep moving
forward.

- Martin Luther King Jr.

Greatness
is not a measure
of how great you
are but how great
others came to be
because of you.

- Cus D'Amato

You have to be proactive about your destiny and then realize that the other half of it is completely out of your control. I think it's fascinating.

- Eric Bana

Believe in your
ability to turn
your dreams
into reality.

- Melissa Le Man

There is no way around hard work. embrace it. You have to put in the hours because there's always something which you can improve.

- Roger Federer

Stop chasing the money and start chasing the passion.

- Tony Hsieh

What one does is what counts and not what one had the intention of doing.

- Pablo Picasso

No matter what
comes your way,
just don't let it
phase you, you can
overcome anything.

- Rose Namajunas

The most rewarding
things you do in life
are often the ones
that look like they
cannot be done.

- Eddie Vedder

Having the strength to tune out negativity and remain focused on what I want gives me the will and confidence to achieve my goals.

- Gisele Bundchen

You will train always for a hundred terrific reasons. Quit and it will be for no good reason at all.

- Dave Draper

It is important to expect nothing, to take every experience, including the negative ones, as merely steps on the path, and to proceed.

- Ram Dass

The secret to my success is practice.

- David Beckham

I think it's imperative to follow your heart and choose a profession you're passionate about, and if you haven't found that 'spark' yet, if you're not sure what you want to do with your lives - be persistent until you do.

- Steve Kerr

In order to lead
the orchestra, you
must first turn your
back to the crowd.

- Mike Mentzer

STAY CONNECTED WITH ME

Social
Instagram: @BrandonMichaelFit
Snapchat: iambrandonfit
YouTube: BrandonMichaelfit

Email
Coaching@BrandonMichaelFit.com

Website
BrandonMichaelFit.com

MORNING

MOTIVATION

Lightning Source UK Ltd.
Milton Keynes UK
UKHW020633100321
380099UK00014B/1360